The Dance Ministry Manual

A Leader's Guide to Starting, Building and Maintaining an Excellent Dance Ministry

Leader's Guide

Kimberly T. Matthews
Renowned Dance Ministry Leader

TheDanceMinistryManual.com

The Dance Ministry Manual

A Leader's Guide to Starting, Building and Maintaining an Excellent Dance Ministry

Leader's Guide

Kimberly T. Matthews
Renowned Dance Ministry Leader

This publication is designed to provide competent and reliable information regarding the subject matter covered. The author and publisher specifically disclaim any liability that is incurred from the use or application of the contents of this book.

If you have purchased this book without a cover, you should be aware that this book may have been stolen property, and reported as unsold and destroyed to the publisher. In such case, neither the author nor the publisher has received any payment for this stripped book.

The Dance Ministry Manual: Leaders Guide
First Edition: © June 2002
by Kimberly T. Matthews
Revised and © February 2014
by Kimberly T. Matthews-Hooker

ISBN 10: 1-943833-07-9
ISBN 13: 978-1-943833-07-8
Published by:
Kissed Publications
PO Box 9819
Hampton, VA 23670

Cover design and interior layout:
Kimberly T. Matthews-Hooker

ABOUT THIS WORKBOOK

The Dance Ministry Manual was originally developed, written and copyrighted in June 2002 by the author of this work as workshop material for the Full Gospel Kingdom Church 1st Annual Holy Convocation. Its original title was *God - The Master and Creator of the Performing Arts,* and the content was found to be so rich and impacting, the material was duplicated several times over and shared throughout the community and east coast and beyond to develop and strengthen dance ministries. As Dance Ministry has evolved and expanded over the years since the original content was written, the material has been further developed to include other aspects of dance and movement ministry.

The goal of this content is to assist dance ministries with becoming ministries of excellence, by providing basic structuring and guidelines for overseeing and participating in dance and movement ministry. It is with the highest level of integrity that, through this manual, this information is now being shared with you. May God <u>always</u> get the glory.

Kimberly T. Matthews

ACKNOWLEDGEMENTS

God is acknowledged in all our ways. It is only through Him that we live move and have our being. He alone is worthy of the praise!

A special thank you goes out to every person who has ever been a member of the Full Gospel Kingdom Church Dance Ministry over the course of nearly two decades. It was because of you and with you that we became a ministry of excellence, and now able to share those practices with others beyond our physical presence. I love every one of you!

LEADER'S NOTES

Use this manual with your group in the way that you feel will serve you best. While each module is arranged in a logical order, you may pick a module that you feel will be most useful and begin there.

Throughout this manual, there are notes included for you that are not in the participant's guides. These notes will guide you as a leader through facilitating the content and activities to your group. Note pages are built in so that you may have participants capture your own teaching, as well as their thoughts.

Makes your sessions interactive, having participants read aloud and participate through demonstration. Feel free to incorporate the physical activities how ever you'd like.

It is strongly suggested that each person in the ministry have their own manual to work from and take notes in. Participant guides can be ordered without enrollment of the online class. Simply go to our website at www.TheDanceMinistryManual.com to place an order. Please do not make copies of any content and distribute it.

You are welcomed to provide any feedback and thoughts about the manual. You may do so by sending an email to info@TheDanceMinsitryManual.com.

Thou hast turned for me my mourning into dancing: thou hast put off my sackcloth, and girded me with gladness

Psalm 30:11

God.
The Master and Creator of the Performing Arts

Participant Workbook
Page 1

TheDanceMinistryManual.com

Leaders Note:

***Page 2 of the Participant's Workbook asks participants to find and write a scripture related to the module.

Find a scripture relating
to this module topic and
write it here:

_____
_____
_____
_____
_____
_____
_____

Leaders Note:

- The **POWER** evoked from an **EARTHQUAKE**
- The display of **MIGHT** seen in a **FLASH OF LIGHTNING**
- The **ADORING WAVE** of **TREE LIMBS** on a breezy day
- The **AUTHORITY** commanded in the fierceness of a **TORNADO**

God – The Master and Creator of the Performing Arts

Participant Workbook Page 3

Of old hast thou laid the foundation of the earth: and the heavens are the work of thy hands. - Psalm 102:25

As God has skillfully created the heavens and the earth with its vast variety of colors, purposes and functions, we are able to see and adore His artwork. In many of His creations, we see how they are able to move, applaud Him, and show forth His glory. Let's visit a few examples:

- The _____ evoked from an _____
- The display of _____ seen in a _____
- The _____ of _____ on a breezy day
- The _____ commanded in the fierceness of a _____

God – The Master and Creator of the Performing Arts

Participant Workbook Page 4

In each of the examples, we find that these creations are able to move and perform. What can you think of that God has created that does **not** move?

_____

Now if you were to leave your home, for an extended or even a brief amount of time, and upon your return you found that your furniture had been shifted about, you would be immediately alarmed. You would want to know what happened while you were away that caused your things to move.

Your home furnishings are man-made; they do not have the ability to move by themselves and should only move if someone or something moves them. We, on the other hand are God-made; and as we discussed, everything God-made moves.

So what a wonderful gift that God has given us, His creation as well, in that we have the ability to move and perform, thus able to take part in His wonderful display of Performing Arts!

Your Own Notes

Participant Workbook Page 5

Leaders Note:

Break your team in groups, or assign a certain number of Creations/Feelings to each member.

Review the list with the group. It's likely that everyone will have some of the same answers. Award points or an award to the group or member who has responses that no one else thought of.

Instruct the group to write down any response they did not come up with on their own.

Consider having a member demonstrate the Creation or the Feeling/Emotion through movement.

God – The Master and Creator of the Performing Arts

Participant Workbook Page 6

Put Your Brain to Work!

Write down at least 50 examples of how God displays his handiwork in the things He has created, along with any feelings or emotions that are evoked with those creations. This exercise will engage your creativity; DON'T STOP until you have listed 50 God-made creations.

Musical Inspiration: Erica Campbell – I'm a Fan

	God's Creation	Feeling/Emotion
1		
2		
3		
4		
5		
6		
7		
8		
9		
10		

TheDanceMinistryManual.com

| Participant Workbook Page 7 | **God – The Master and Creator of the Performing Arts** |

	God's Creation	Feeling/Emotion
11		
12		
13		
14		
15		
16		
17		
18		
19		
20		
21		
22		
23		
24		
25		
26		

God – The Master and Creator of the Performing Arts

Participant Workbook Page 8

	God's Creation	Feeling/Emotion
27		
28		
29		
30		
31		
32		
33		
34		
35		
36		
37		
38		
39		
40		
41		
42		

Participant Workbook Page 9

God – The Master and Creator of the Performing Arts

	God's Creation	Feeling/Emotion
43		
44		
45		
46		
47		
48		
49		
50		

Isn't God Amazing?

Jot down any new, fresh or exciting revelations you received or learned about God, The Master Creator, while you worked on this exercise.

_____
_____
_____
_____
_____
_____

The Dance Ministry

Participant Workbook Page 11

***Page 12 of the Participant's Workbook asks participants to find and write a scripture related to the module.**

Thou hast turned for me my mourning into dancing: thou hast put off my sackcloth, and girded me with gladness

Psalm 30:11

The Dance Ministry	Participant Workbook Page 13

Thou hast turned for me my mourning into dancing: thou hast put off my sackcloth, and girded me with gladness. - Psalm 30:11

The ministry of dance/mime/movement is a powerful and exciting ministry of performing arts in which we are able to worship and display our love for God in our movements and expressions. The Bible clearly instructs us to praise God in dance, for example:

- _____

- _____

While any of us with the ability to move our limbs can dance before Him, we know that God fashions things to not only function individually, but to also work together to bring Him glory.

We're going to discuss the dance ministry in terms of functioning as a group, and working collaboratively together.

Leaders Note:

It is not…

- **A weight loss regimen**

- **A tone up program**

- **A meet up for friends**

- **Something to do for fun**

The Dance Ministry

Participant Workbook Page 14

Now before we look at some key components of what the Dance Ministry is, let's first think about what the Dance Ministry is NOT.

It is not…

- _____
- _____
- _____
- _____

Dance Ministry is just that – ministry! Those involved in a Dance Ministry are in a position to impact the lives of those who are hurting, in need of encouragement, needing to hear from God, and/or seeking salvation, just to mention a few things.

This ministry, as any other, is one that requires constant prayer, dedication, commitment, and desire to want to not just minister to God, but to God's people. As the ministry consistently seeks God for direction, revelation, creativity, what to minister, and how to minister, not only will the execution of the ministry grow, but also the spiritual life of each individual will become stronger.

Leader's Notes and Observations

The Wave Zone

Participant Workbook
Page 15

Leaders Note:

***Page 16 of the Participant's Workbook asks participants to find and write a scripture related to the module.**

Before starting this module, have dancers improv while you observe.

Make a note of any body parts that are not engaged, then share that feedback.

_____
_____
_____
_____
_____
_____
_____
_____
_____
_____
_____
_____
_____
_____
_____

After you have provided feedback on your observations, watch for improvement or implementation of your feedback.

THE WAVE ZONE

Participant Workbook Page 17

The Wave Zone

When we see a physically challenged person, what is it about that person that signals to us that he or she has a limitation? Most often, it is the lack of movement of a specific part of his or her body. Even if it is as small as a finger that does not bend at the knuckle like it's suppose to, we take notice of that limitation, and it registers in our minds as a handicap.

Too many times in dance ministry, dancers get stuck in The Wave Zone, where the choreography is limited to simple waving motions, leaving the rest of the body to be perceived as disabled. This is a tremendous oversight of God's gift of movement to us.

Consider that even when a person is unfortunately, bound to a wheelchair, he or she will still maneuver the chair about to express dancing. With that said, there is no reason why, when we have no physical limitations, we should be trapped in The Wave Zone.

Now you may not be able to do a triple pirouette and end it with a Firebird leap today, but certainly, you can enhance your movements further than just waving and pointing. Explore your body's movement capabilities and recognize the amazing things you can do.

Leaders Note:

Have members list various ways their body can move. This is a great place to introduce or reinforce dance terms.

- Run
- Hop
- Skip
- Jump
- Fall
- Lay
- Turn

Consider having dancers demonstrate some of the movement.

THE WAVE ZONE

Participant Workbook Page 18

Don't get stuck in The Wave Zone! First, write down the scripture noted below, then make an extensive list of everything you can do with your body to express movement. Be sure to fill in every blank! If you get stuck, research some dance terminology!

Psalm 95:4-5

_____
_____
_____
_____
_____

Thank you Lord for giving me the ability to:

Leader's Notes and Observations

The Power of Dance and Movement

Participant Workbook Page 19

Leaders Note:

***Page 20 of the Participant's Workbook asks participants to find and write a scripture related to the module.

Have members read the below passage of scripture from their bibles. *Matthew 14:3-9 King James Version (KJV)*

3 For Herod had laid hold on John, and bound him, and put him in prison for Herodias' sake, his brother Philip's wife.

4 For John said unto him, It is not lawful for thee to have her.

5 And when he would have put him to death, he feared the multitude, because they counted him as a prophet.

6 But when Herod's birthday was kept, the daughter of Herodias danced before them, and pleased Herod.

7 Whereupon he promised with an oath to give her whatsoever she would ask.

8 And she, being before instructed of her mother, said, Give me here John Baptist's head in a charger.

9 And the king was sorry: nevertheless for the oath's sake, and them which sat with him at meat, he commanded it to be given her.

Facilitate a discussion about what was read.

Leaders Note:

List the scriptures you want to bring to your team's attention.

_____
_____
_____
_____
_____
_____
_____
_____
_____
_____
_____
_____
_____
_____
_____

Participant Workbook Page 21

The Power of Dance And Movement

Search The Scriptures

What references to dance are you able to find in the bible? Write them down, then, write for what purpose was dance being utilized.

Verse:
_____
_____
_____
_____
_____
_____
_____

Purpose:
_____
_____

Verse:
_____
_____
_____
_____
_____
_____

Purpose:
_____
_____

The Power of Dance And Movement

Participant Workbook Page 22

Verse:
_____
_____
_____
_____
_____
_____

Purpose:
_____
_____

Verse:
_____
_____
_____
_____
_____
_____

Purpose:
_____
_____

Participant Workbook Page 23

The Power of Dance And Movement

Verse:
_____
_____
_____
_____
_____
_____

Purpose:
_____
_____

Verse:
_____
_____
_____
_____
_____
_____

Purpose:
_____
_____

The Power of Dance And Movement

Participant Workbook Page 24

Verse:
_____
_____
_____
_____
_____
_____

Purpose:
_____
_____

Verse:
_____
_____
_____
_____
_____
_____

Purpose:
_____
_____

Leader's Notes and Observations

Excellence.
What Do You
Mean By That?

Participant
Workbook
Page 25

Leaders Note:

***Page 26 of the Participant's Workbook asks participants to find and write a scripture related to the module.**

Facilitate a discussion about what does it mean to be excellent. Expand beyond dance and movement. Have your members think about things that re not ministry related such as:

- A restaurant
- A shopping experience
- A customer service experience
- A Concert

Encourage the group to explain what made those experiences excellent.

You may want to split the group up for this exercise for collaborative thinking, or just assign one person to list one or two groups along with those groups' Qualities of Excellence.

What Do You Mean by That?	Participant Workbook Page 27

O Lord our Lord, how excellent is thy name in all the earth. ~ Psalm 8:9

Think Outside of Yourself

Are there other ministries, dance groups or performance teams you've seen that you consider to be excellent? Make a list of at least ten of them. As you write down their group names, include a brief summary of how that has equated to excellence to you. Be specific and again, do not skip through this exercise. Take the time and thought needed to work through it completely.

Group's Name: _____

Qualities of Excellence:
_____
_____
_____

Group's Name: _____

Qualities of Excellence:
_____
_____
_____

Participant Workbook Page 28

What Do You Mean by That?

Group's Name: _____

Qualities of Excellence:
_____
_____
_____

Group's Name: _____

Qualities of Excellence:
_____
_____
_____

Group's Name: _____

Qualities of Excellence:
_____
_____
_____

Group's Name: _____

Qualities of Excellence:
_____
_____
_____

What Do You Mean by That?

Participant Workbook Page 29

Group's Name: _____

Qualities of Excellence:
_____
_____
_____

Group's Name: _____

Qualities of Excellence:
_____
_____
_____

Group's Name: _____

Qualities of Excellence:
_____
_____
_____

Group's Name: _____

Qualities of Excellence:
_____
_____
_____

Participant Workbook Page 30

What Do You Mean by That?

What About Your Team?

From the details you noted on your group observations, you should be able to easily identify what excellence means, and looks like to you. Compile those qualities into a list here, then rate on a scale of 1-5 how you feel your team rates for each quality.

Quality of Excellence	1-5 Ranking

What Do You Mean by That?

Participant Workbook Page 31

All The Way Around

Don't limit your thoughts to just performance; define excellence for every aspect of your ministry. What does an excellent rehearsal look like? How about team dynamics? Think through all aspects and get clear on your vision of excellence.

Area: _____

My vision of excellence is:
_____
_____
_____
_____
_____

Area: _____

My vision of excellence is:
_____
_____
_____
_____
_____

| Participant Workbook Page 32 | **What Do You Mean by That?** |

Area: _____

My vision of excellence is:
_____
_____
_____
_____
_____

Area: _____

My vision of excellence is:
_____
_____
_____
_____
_____

Area: _____

My vision of excellence is:
_____
_____
_____
_____
_____

What Do You Bring To The Ministry

Participant Workbook Page 33

Leaders Note:

***Page 34 of the Participant's Workbook asks participants to find and write a scripture related to the module.**

Have members read the below passage of scripture from their bibles.

Matthew 25:15a
And unto one he gave five talents, to another two, and to another one; to every man according to his several ability;

Facilitate a discussion about what was read.

Leaders Note:

Facilitate a discussion about talent, skill and support. Ask why each element is important.

Discuss what can happen when things are not properly supported.

What do You Bring To the Ministry

Participant Workbook Page 35

Take a few minutes to think about what you contribute to your team. In what area can the leader most depend on you? In what area do you struggle? Write your thoughts below:

My greatest contribution to the dance ministry is:
_____
_____
_____
_____

My leader can also depend on me to:
_____
_____
_____
_____

I could really use some help with:
_____
_____
_____
_____

Participant Workbook Page 36

How Do You View Your Team

Now take the next several minutes to think of the members of your dance ministry. List each person, and beside his or her name, write down what you admire about that person as it relates to the dance ministry, or how that person best supports the team. Be ready to share your responses.

_____ is **great** at
_____
_____

_____ is **awesome** with
_____
_____

I really **appreciate** _____
because _____
_____
_____

_____ **impresses** me
by _____
_____

How Do You View Your Team

Participant Workbook Page 37

_____ is **great** at
_____
_____

_____ is **awesome** with
_____
_____

I really **appreciate** _____
because _____
_____
_____

_____ **impresses** me
by _____
_____

_____ is **amazing** at
_____
_____

TheDanceMinistryManual.com

> **Participant Workbook Page 38**
>
> **What Do You Bring To The Ministry**

Talent and Skill:

While some have had formal dance training, many individuals possess the natural talent, ability and coordination to dance. Because of this, formal dance training is not necessary. Of course if there is someone who has had formal training, that individual can help to develop the skill of others. If one is willing to learn, and has the spirit of submission, excellence, and servitude, combined with some natural ability, God can and will provide the rest.

Support

As your team grows and develops, you will find that some people excel in support, and you will need lots of that. That person (or few) may not dance well, but they are excellent in ensuring praise garments are cleaned and ironed, (if team members are not individually responsible for maintaining garments). The support person doesn't mind communicating with the sound person on the day you minister, while you get dressed and do other things. The support person won't mind assisting with creating props, looking for missing garments, stopping at the store to pick up something you need, researching a particular product etc. These people are very valuable to any ministry, dance ministry included.

Leaders Note:

After members have completed their assessments of themselves, have them share with the group what they feel each other's contributions are. This will help them to develop an appreciation for each other's contributions to the team.

Share your notes as well to confirm or add to their list of contributions.

Participant Workbook Page 39

What Do You Bring To The Ministry

Think through what your individual contributions are to your ministry as a whole. Not just leadership, but how can your team members, your church and your community most depend on you. What about areas you struggle with? Take the time to identify what you bring, and then what each of your team members bring to the ministry.

As for me:
My greatest contribution to the dance ministry is:
_____
_____
_____
_____

My church can depend on me to:
_____
_____
_____
_____

But I could really use some help with:
_____
_____
_____
_____

Now, on the next pages, complete the statements for every member of your team.

What Do You Bring To The Ministry

Participant Workbook Page 40

Name: _____

Greatest contribution to the dance ministry is:
_____
_____
_____
_____

Can be depended upon to:
_____
_____
_____
_____

An area of growth is:
_____
_____
_____
_____

How would your ministry be impacted if this individual were no longer involved in the ministry?
_____
_____
_____
_____

Participant Workbook Page 41

What Do You Bring To The Ministry

Name: _____

Greatest contribution to the dance ministry is:
_____
_____
_____
_____

Can be depended upon to:
_____
_____
_____
_____

An area of growth is:
_____
_____
_____
_____

How would your ministry be impacted if this individual were no longer involved in the ministry?
_____
_____
_____
_____

TheDanceMinistryManual.com

What Do You Bring To The Ministry

Participant Workbook Page 42

Name: _____

Greatest contribution to the dance ministry is:
_____
_____
_____
_____

Can be depended upon to:
_____
_____
_____
_____

An area of growth is:
_____
_____
_____
_____

How would your ministry be impacted if this individual were no longer involved in the ministry?
_____
_____
_____
_____

Participant Workbook Page 43

What Do You Bring To The Ministry

Name: _____

Greatest contribution to the dance ministry is:
_____
_____
_____
_____

Can be depended upon to:
_____
_____
_____
_____

An area of growth is:
_____
_____
_____
_____

How would your ministry be impacted if this individual were no longer involved in the ministry?
_____
_____
_____
_____

What Do You Bring To The Ministry

Participant Workbook Page 44

Name: _____

Greatest contribution to the dance ministry is:
_____
_____
_____
_____

Can be depended upon to:
_____
_____
_____
_____

An area of growth is:
_____
_____
_____
_____

How would your ministry be impacted if this individual were no longer involved in the ministry?
_____
_____
_____
_____

Participant Workbook Page 45

What Do You Bring To The Ministry

Name: _____

Greatest contribution to the dance ministry is:
_____
_____
_____
_____

Can be depended upon to:
_____
_____
_____
_____

An area of growth is:
_____
_____
_____
_____

How would your ministry be impacted if this individual were no longer involved in the ministry?
_____
_____
_____
_____

Building a Well-Rounded Team

Participant Workbook Page 47

Leaders Note:

***Page 48 of the Participant's Workbook asks participants to find and write a scripture related to the module.**

Have members read the below passage of scripture from their bibles.

I Corinthians 12:21
And the eye cannot say unto the hand, I have no need of thee: nor again the head to the feet, I have no need of you

Facilitate a discussion about what was read.

Determine your guidelines and write them below prior to facilitating.

Individuals should also:

- _____

- _____

- _____

- _____

- _____

Building a Well-Rounded Ministry

Participant Workbook Page 49

Core Qualities:
Individuals interested in being a part of the dance ministry should sincerely desire to worship and praise God in dance, have (or in the process of developing) a heart for God's people, a supporter of the leader's vision, and/or able to submit to authority and commit to the vision.

Individuals should also:

- _____
- _____
- _____
- _____
- _____

Participant Workbook Page 50	**Building a Well-Rounded Ministry**

Suppose your paycheck depended on it?

Think outside of the ministry box for a minute, and think from the perspective of a business owner or manager. You own a dance school and have three job positions to fill on your team and a large stack of applications. Selecting the best candidates will result in increased student enrollment and parent satisfaction, which would mean a larger paycheck for you. What qualities would you look for to help you make the best hiring decision?

Think of 24 qualities you would want your selected candidates to have. DO NOT cheat by leaving blank spaces.

	Quality		Quality		Quality
1		9		17	
2		10		18	
3		11		19	
4		12		20	
5		13		21	
6		14		22	
7		15		23	
8		16		24	

Building a Well-Rounded Ministry	Participant Workbook Page 51

Evaluate Your List:
Now review your list and take note of how many of the qualities are purely skill related, and how many are not skill related at all but are equally, if not more important.

Rank Your List:
Refer to your list from the previous page and identify the top six qualities that you determine to be most important, then write why that particular quality is important.

1. _____
   _____
   _____

2. _____
   _____
   _____

3. _____
   _____
   _____

Participant Workbook Page 52
Building a Well-Rounded Ministry

4. _____

5. _____

6. _____

Leaders Note:

Have members read the below passage of scripture from their bibles.

And whatsoever ye do, do it heartily, as to the Lord, and not unto men; ~ Colossians 3:23

Facilitate a discussion about what was read

Participant Workbook Page 53

What's Your Motivation?

What Motivates You?

I joined the dance ministry because:
_____
_____

I continue to be a part of the ministry because:
_____
_____

What is most rewarding for me about being on the dance ministry is:
_____
_____

If the decision was made to "shut down" the dance ministry, I would feel:
_____
_____

The reason I would feel that way is:
_____
_____

The dance ministry adds value to my church's vision and mission by:
_____
_____

What's Your Motivation?

Participant Workbook Page 54

What discoveries have you made about your team or yourself through this exercise?

_____
_____
_____
_____
_____

Do you feel that your team's attitude about the dance ministry is reflected when you minister?

_____
_____
_____
_____
_____

What can you do to shift the your motivations to those more conducive to ministry service (if a shift is needed)?

_____
_____
_____
_____
_____

Leader's Notes and Observations

Auditioning

Participant Workbook Page 55

Leaders Note:

***Page 56 of the Participant's Workbook asks participants to find and write a scripture related to the module.**

Ask members to share how they have joined other teams, organizations, groups or even jobs.

Point out that most places have a process to take on new members, and joining, most times extends far beyond expressing interest.

Auditioning for Your Ministry

Participant Workbook Page 57

How Do They Join?

Think about various teams/clubs/organizations and how they acquire new members. Is there a formal process? Make notes of what you know their formal processes to be. Be as detailed as you can.

Team/Organization: _____

Joining Process: _____

_____

_____

_____

Team/Organization: _____

Joining Process: _____

_____

_____

_____

Participant Workbook Page 58 — Auditioning for Your Ministry

Team/Organization: _____

Joining Process: _____

_____

_____

_____

Team/Organization: _____

Joining Process: _____

_____

_____

_____

Team/Organization: _____

Joining Process: _____

_____

_____

_____

Auditioning for Your Ministry

Participant Workbook Page 59

There are very few organizations in which a person can just simply express interest and be allowed to participate. In the way of sports, there are generally tryouts. When a high school student desires to attend a particular college, she has to apply, write an essay, get recommendation letters and a few other things in order to be considered for acceptance. An actor who wants a part in a play, has to present his talent before a director prior to being assigned a role. Employers require interviews and in most instances resumes.

But this is church!

Some may feel that auditioning is "too much" and should not be a part of a ministry process, but let's look at a Biblical reference point, the manner in which Esther came to be Queen.

Participant Workbook Page 60

Auditioning for Your Ministry

1: After these things, when the wrath of king Ahasuerus was appeased, he remembered Vashti, and what she had done, and what was decreed against her.

2: Then said the king's servants that ministered unto him, Let there be fair young virgins sought for the king:

3: And let the king appoint officers in all the provinces of his kingdom, that they may gather together all the fair young virgins unto Shushan the palace, to the house of the women, unto the custody of Hege the king's chamberlain, keeper of the women; and let their things for purification be given them:

4: And let the maiden which pleaseth the king be queen instead of Vashti. And the thing pleased the king; and he did so.

8: So it came to pass, when the king's commandment and his decree was heard, and when many maidens were gathered together unto Shushan the palace, to the custody of Hegai, that Esther was brought also unto the king's house, to the custody of Hegai, keeper of the women.

9: And the maiden pleased him, and she obtained kindness of him; and he speedily gave her her things for purification, with such things as belonged to her, and seven maidens, which were meet to be given her, out of the king's house: and he preferred her and her maids unto the best place of the house of the women.

10: Esther had not shewed her people nor her kindred: for Mordecai had charged her that she should not shew it.

11: And Mordecai walked every day before the court of the women's house, to know how Esther did, and what should become of her.

Auditioning for Your Ministry

Participant Workbook Page 61

12: Now when every maid's turn was come to go in to king Ahasuerus, after that she had been twelve months, according to the manner of the women, (for so were the days of their purifications accomplished, to wit, six months with oil of myrrh, and six months with sweet odours, and with other things for the purifying of the women;)

13: Then thus came every maiden unto the king; whatsoever she desired was given her to go with her out of the house of the women unto the king's house.

14 In the evening she went, and on the morrow she returned into the second house of the women, to the custody of Shaashgaz, the king's chamberlain, which kept the concubines: she came in unto the king no more, except the king delighted in her, and that she were called by name.

15: Now when the turn of Esther, the daughter of Abihail the uncle of Mordecai, who had taken her for his daughter, was come to go in unto the king, she required nothing but what Hegai the king's chamberlain, the keeper of the women, appointed. And Esther obtained favour in the sight of all them that looked upon her.

16: So Esther was taken unto king Ahasuerus into his house royal in the tenth month, which is the month Tebeth, in the seventh year of his reign.

17: And the king loved Esther above all the women, and she obtained grace and favour in his sight more than all the virgins; so that he set the royal crown upon her head, and made her queen instead of Vashti.

As you see, Esther did not become Queen by happenstance or just because she expressed a desire that she was interested in the role, or even that she had received a word from the Lord, or a calling in her spirit. Although, we know it was the hand of God that placed Esther in that position, His methods for having Esther selected was similar to an audition, for which she had to properly prepare; there was a formal process.

Leaders Note:

Point out that one of the criteria for a woman to have been considered for queen was that she had to be a virgin.

Facilitate a discussion about what criteria should be met for a person to be involved in the ministry. Be sure to ask members why the criteria is important.

Auditioning for Your Ministry

Participant Workbook Page 62

The criteria for being a part of the ministry should be clearly defined. This will help interested individuals to properly prepare to join and enhance the team.

- Does a person need to be a member of your church?
- Is there an age requirement or limit?
- Must those who are students maintain a certain grade point average?
- Is Bible Study attendance necessary?

Define your requirements below, and write out why it is necessary that members meet it. If you can't explain why a certain requirement is necessary, rethink it; maybe it shouldn't be a requirement at all.

_____
_____
_____

_____
_____
_____

_____
_____
_____

Participant Workbook Page 63 — **Auditioning for Your Ministry**

Leaders Note:

Panel Auditioning is a practice utilized for a few reasons; it provides:

- <u>An Upfront Assessment</u>

A panel will be able to tell if a person has a good sense of rhythm, timing, coordination, skill, creativity, variety of movement, etc.

- <u>An Unbiased Selection Process</u>

Because there will be more than one person on the audition panel, it prevents a person being selected or rejected based on personal opinion.

- <u>Demonstrated Desire to Join</u>

Auditions can be intimidating, but someone who really wants to be a part of the ministry won't mind demonstrating that desire with her/his best effort.

Participant Workbook Page 64 — **Auditioning for Your Ministry**

Panel Auditioning is a great idea for a few reasons; it provides:

_____
_____
_____
_____
_____
_____
_____
_____

_____
_____
_____
_____
_____
_____
_____
_____

_____
_____
_____
_____
_____
_____
_____
_____

Leaders Note:

The auditions are very thorough, asking each candidate to:

1. Present prepared choreography
2. Replicate demonstrated choreography
3. Improv on the spot

Each piece is very important as dance team members are selected. One may possess the SKILL/TALENT, but lack the CREATIVITY which would be discovered in the PRESENTATION portion of the audition.

Another may have CREATIVITY but is unable to quickly learn the choreography necessary to execute an existing routine, which would be discovered in the REPLICATION portion.

Another may be able to pick up the CHOREOGRAPHY but can't EXECUTE IT WITH EXCELLENCE.

Participant Workbook Page 65

Auditioning for Your Ministry

The auditions are very thorough, asking each candidate to:

① ② ③

Each piece is very important as dance team members are selected. One may possess _____, but lack the _____ _____ which would be discovered in the _____ portion of the audition. Another may have _____ but is unable to quickly learn the choreography necessary to execute an existing routine, which would be discovered in the _____ _____ portion. Another may be able to pick up the _____ but can't _____.

The absence of any one of these things do not expressly mean the person is not a good fit for the team, but it will expose right away where a person's strengths and growth areas are. Through the audition process, all of this can be assessed up-front to ensure that the ministry will be well rounded, possessing the skill, talent and ability to effectively minister.

Leaders Note:

Have your team think through who would be good to have on an audition panel and why.

Participant Workbook Page 66

Auditioning for Your Ministry

Who would you choose to sit on the audition panel, and why? Should only those with dance experience be included? Should you consider someone who is not involved in the music ministry at all?

_____
_____
_____
_____
_____
_____
_____
_____
_____
_____
_____
_____
_____
_____

> **Leaders Note:**
>
> Facilitate a discussion with your team to determine what process would be the right choice for your ministry.

> **Participant Workbook Page 67**
>
> **Auditioning for Your Ministry**

What process do you currently have in place?

Now that you have thought through the details of how other organizations acquire new members, are you able to identify any similarities that stand out?

_____

_____

_____

Is this something you can implement in your ministry? If yes, how would it help you to select and maintain your members?

_____

_____

_____

What other processes would be advantageous to include as you look to build or expand your team?

_____

_____

_____

Auditioning for Your Ministry

Participant Workbook Page 68

Develop Your Questioning Strategy

Create 20 questions that would be beneficial to ask your candidates in an interview format.

_____
_____
_____
_____
_____
_____
_____
_____
_____
_____
_____
_____
_____
_____

Participant Workbook Page 69 — **Auditioning for Your Ministry**

Auditioning for Your Ministry

Participant Workbook Page 70

Take notes on each ministry candidate.

Here is a simple format you can use to take notes on your ministry candidates' auditions. Some things you may want to look for are:

Did the candidate start when the music started, or waited until a certain part of the song? How well was the choreography executed? Did the candidate engage her whole body, or was she confined to The Wave Zone?

Your notes should be detailed and specific, so that you can provide solid feedback to your candidate.

Candidate's Name: _____

Song Presented: _____

Strengths:
_____
_____

Opportunities for Growth:
_____
_____

Participant Workbook Page 71 — **Auditioning for Your Ministry**

Pre-Choreographed Presentation:
_____
_____
_____

Improvisation:
_____
_____
_____

On-the-Spot Choreography:
_____
_____
_____

| Auditioning for Your Ministry | Participant Workbook Page 72 |

What contribution do you feel you will add to the ministry?
_____
_____
_____

Where do you think you would need the most help?
_____
_____
_____

What other ministries interest you, and how will you prioritize between them?
_____
_____
_____

Feel free to implement any question (s) you developed on the previous dance doc.

Participant Workbook Page 73

How Can the Ministry Improve

It is also very important that you are able to identify and address any areas where your ministry needs to improve. Take a few minutes to think of how individually, or collectively the team can go from good to great, and better to best!

Practice Makes Perfect

Participant Workbook Page 75

***Page 76 of the Participant's Workbook asks participants to find and write a scripture related to the module.**

Study to shew thyself approved unto God, a workman that needeth not to be ashamed, rightly dividing the word of truth.

2 Timothy 2:15

Practice Makes Perfect

Participant Workbook Page 77

Study to shew thyself approved unto God, a workman that needeth not to be ashamed . . . - 2 Tim 2:15

Regularly scheduled rehearsals are key in developing a dance ministry. We cannot make the mistake of only practicing when something needs to be accomplished. This does not allow for skill and talent to be developed or perfected.

Rehearsals must be consistent and ongoing in order for the ministry to thrive successfully. Even if the team is not working on a particular routine or piece, it is important to continue to meet, rehearse, and practice consistently. The focus can be changed from working on a routine, to working on technical dance movements, strength and endurance training, fellowshipping, sharing from the word, or discussing matters that impact the ministry such as upcoming dates/events, or even creating props.

Arrive to practice on time and ready to practice. Leave your problems, trials and stressors at the door, and come in with a thankful and grateful heart and attitude. Even if you've had a not-so-great day, thank God that you made it through and His mercy is abundant.

Practice Makes Perfect

Participant Workbook Page 78

As mentioned previously, prayer is a vital and necessary component for the success of not just the dance ministry, but any ministry. There must be a leader who has a solid relationship with God and is able to hear and receive from Him regarding His plan, desire, and purposes for the ministry. Begin each rehearsal with prayer.

Each rehearsal should include a full warm-up, properly preparing the body for physical activity, generally led by a skilled team member. The warm-up may be skill based, simple stretches, and/or involve cardiovascular exercises. If no one is particularly skilled in this area, consider using an exercise DVD for this portion. There are plenty available to choose from.

Depending upon the complexity of the routines or goal being work towards, the team may work on one or two routines during a rehearsal over an hour's time. Afterward a cool down is led and the rehearsal should close with prayer.

Practice Makes Perfect

Participant Workbook Page 79

Prayer/Meditation: - from the time each person arrives to 5 mins after your rehearsal start time. Have each dancer take a specific stretch pose (or one of their choosing), and meditate on scripture or the lyrics to a song you may want to work on, or spend time in quiet prayer. End this portion with an opening group prayer.

Cardio Warm Up: Turn on your favorite upbeat song and begin moving your feet and body. Vary the movements, making sure to include footwork or movement that may be in your choreography.

Stretch Session: Guide the team through a full body stretch, to further warm up the body and increase flexibility.

Crossing the Floor: Have dancers repeat a specific movement, or a series of movements all the way across the room and back. If you practice in a narrow sanctuary, use the aisle. Repetition will strengthen skill.

Improvisation: Turn on some music and just let the group dance! One person at a time, a few at a time, or the entire group at once. There are no hard or fast rules, other than to keep dancing.

Creativity Builders: Incorporate an exercise that fosters creative thinking in choreography. See the bonus Dance Doc on Creativity Builders for ideas.

> **Participant Workbook Page 80**
>
> **Practice Makes Perfect**

Choreography: In this portion of your rehearsal, focus on creating new, freshening, reviewing or cleaning up choreography.

Open Items: Address any team business, upcoming engagements, housekeeping, reminders etc.

Closing Prayer: Close your rehearsal with prayer, thanking God for all that was accomplished in the session.

Practice Makes Perfect

Participant Workbook Page 81

Rehearsal Checklist: How many of these elements are present in your current rehearsal structure? While it may not be ideal to have every component at every rehearsal, which ones do you need to implement in order to grow your ministry to excellence? Which will you implement to be included in EVERY rehearsal? Circle your responses.

- **Prayer** -   occasionally or every time

- **Meditation** - occasionally or every time

- **Cardio Warm Up** - occasionally or every time

- **Stretch Session** - occasionally or every time

- **Crossing the Floor** - occasionally or every time

- **Improvisation** - occasionally or every time

- **Creativity Builders** - occasionally or every time

- **Choreography** - occasionally or every time

- **Open Items/Discussion** - occasionally or every time

- **Closing Prayer** - occasionally or every time

Participant Workbook Page 82

Practice Makes Perfect

Create Your Revamped Practice Agenda:

Outline how much time will be spent on each portion of your rehearsal. You may want to start by completing the total time you generally spend in your regular rehearsals, then allot minutes from there.

Rehearsal Activity	Suggested Time	Actual Time
Prayer/Meditation	5	
Cardio Warm-Up	30	
Full Body Stretch	10	
Crossing the Floor	30	
Improvisation	30	
Creativity Builders	30	
Choreography	60	
Open Items	10	
Other Activities	30	
Closing Prayer	2	
Total Time:	**238 mins**	

A Creative Anointing

Participant Workbook Page 83

***Page 84 of the Participant's Workbook asks participants to find and write a scripture related to the module.

Thus saith God the LORD, he that created the heavens, and stretched them out; he that spread forth the earth, and that which cometh out of it; he that giveth breath unto the people upon it, and spirit to them that walk therein:

Isaiah 42:5

| A Creative Anointing | Participant Workbook Page 85 |

We've already explored the fact that God is a Master Creator, as a matter of fact, it is the very first thing the Bible reveals about God:

In the beginning God created . . . Genesis 1:1

and it is obvious that His creativity is amazing! Just take a look at some of His work.

Participant Workbook Page 86

A Creative Anointing

Write your thoughts about each of the images

1. _____
   _____

2. _____
   _____

3. _____
   _____

4. _____
   _____

5. _____
   _____

6. _____
   _____

7. _____
   _____

8. _____
   _____

9. _____
   _____

A Creative Anointing

Participant Workbook Page 87

His work is amazing, wouldn't you agree?

The Bible says we are made in God's image and in his likeness. Fashioned after Him and made like Him, so while our creativity will never match what He is able to do, we certainly have the creative power within us. This gift of creativity is wonderfully exciting and powerful when it comes to dance ministry.

You and your team should pray for a creative anointing for your ministry. Creativity is what will set your ministry apart from others. It will help you to demonstrate and convey the message in your movement in a far more engaging way.

Get ready to super work your brain in this next activity!

Leaders Note:

Choose the songs you want to play for your group, or ask your group to select songs.

You may want to pair team members together to foster collaborative thinking.

After the team has an opportunity to create scripts, have them share with the group. Ask the group to visualize the scenes and share their thoughts of how well the story line and the music pair.

A Creative Anointing

Participant Workbook Page 88

Have you ever watched a particular scene in a movie, which was perfectly enhanced by an accompanying soundtrack? What do you think happened first – the movie script was written, then appropriate music was selected, or do you think it happened the other way around?

The actors didn't adjust the scene for the music, but inversely, the music fit the scene, and thereby, evoked a greater emotional tie-in for the viewers. Think of the choreography you create in ministry that same way.

How many times have you heard a song writer say something like:

"I was going through a tough season in my life, and I didn't know what to do or where to turn, and God gave me this song."

That is another example of what is meant by the song enhancing the story. The songwriter didn't write the song first, then go through the experience to match. It was the other way around. It will take some practice and some brainstorming, but if you begin to work your choreography from a visionary standpoint, it will become easier to create ministry presentations that make a greater and more powerful impact to the congregation and/or audience.

Participant Workbook Page 89

A Creative Anointing

Write a Movie Script:

List 7 of your favorite songs, ensuring that they vary in tempo, tone, musicality etc. Also, pick songs that you or your team have not previously choreographed.

1. _____
2. _____
3. _____
4. _____
5. _____
6. _____
7. _____

Close your eyes and listen to your first song selection. As you listen, imagine that the song is included on the sound track for a movie script. For that song, create a movie plot, imagining that the song correlates with the movie's theme, write what the plot of the movie is, and what is going on in the scene for which your song of choice is being played. Repeat this for every song on your list.

A Creative Anointing	Participant Workbook Page 90

Movie One:

Movie Title: _____

Theme Song (from your list): _____

Movie Plot: _____
_____
_____
_____
_____
_____
_____
_____

Describe in detail the scene for which the song plays:
_____
_____
_____
_____
_____
_____
_____
_____
_____
_____
_____
_____
_____
_____

Participant Workbook Page 91   **A Creative Anointing**

Movie Two:

Movie Title: _____

Theme Song (from your list): _____

Movie Plot: _____
_____
_____
_____
_____
_____
_____
_____
_____

Describe in detail the scene for which the song plays:
_____
_____
_____
_____
_____
_____
_____
_____
_____
_____
_____
_____
_____

A Creative Anointing	Participant Workbook Page 92

Movie Three:

Movie Title: _____

Theme Song (from your list): _____

Movie Plot: _____
_____
_____
_____
_____
_____
_____
_____

Describe in detail the scene for which the song plays:
_____
_____
_____
_____
_____
_____
_____
_____
_____
_____
_____
_____
_____
_____

Participant Workbook Page 93

A Creative Anointing

Movie Four:

Movie Title: _____

Theme Song (from your list): _____

Movie Plot: _____
_____
_____
_____
_____
_____
_____
_____
_____

Describe in detail the scene for which the song plays:
_____
_____
_____
_____
_____
_____
_____
_____
_____
_____
_____
_____
_____
_____

A Creative Anointing	Participant Workbook Page 94

Movie Five:

Movie Title: _____

Theme Song (from your list): _____

Movie Plot: _____
_____
_____
_____
_____
_____
_____

Describe in detail the scene for which the song plays:
_____
_____
_____
_____
_____
_____
_____
_____
_____
_____
_____
_____
_____

| Participant Workbook Page 95 | **A Creative Anointing** |

Movie Six:

Movie Title: _____

Theme Song (from your list): _____

Movie Plot: _____
_____
_____
_____
_____
_____
_____
_____
_____

Describe in detail the scene for which the song plays:
_____
_____
_____
_____
_____
_____
_____
_____
_____
_____
_____
_____
_____
_____

A Creative Anointing	Participant Workbook Page 96

Movie Seven:

Movie Title: _____

Theme Song (from your list): _____

Movie Plot: _____
_____
_____
_____
_____
_____
_____
_____

Describe in detail the scene for which the song plays:
_____
_____
_____
_____
_____
_____
_____
_____
_____
_____
_____
_____
_____

Leader's Notes and Observations

Amazing Choreography That Tells A Story

Participant Workbook Page 97

***Page 98 of the Participant's Workbook asks participants to find and write a scripture related to the module.

Let them praise his name in the dance: let them sing praises unto him with the timbrel and harp.

Psalm 149:3

What Story Does Your Choreography Tell?

Participant Workbook Page 99

Many times, dance ministries present choreography that is simplified to not much more than the waving of hands and pointing. It is easy to slip into this style of routine creation, because most often, routines are inspired by lyrics. Combine that with a lack of creative thinking, and the result is, a simple upwards point to convey God, crossed arms over the chest for love, and a point in the direction of the congregation to demonstrate the word "you." Then add to that, a step to the left and a step to the right, if any footwork is added at all.

Again, consider that God is the Master and Creator of the performing arts. Reflect again on how beautiful, and breathtakingly amazing His works are. Now remember that you are made in His image and you possess that same creative nature. Creativity may not be your strength, but you do have creative talent, and can find someone who is strong in that area to support the ministry.

Too often we let the song tell the story, and attempt to enhance the song with choreography, but I challenge you to reverse this thinking. Let your **choreography** tell the story, and let the song enhance it.

> Leaders Note:
>
> Have your group watch one or two of your ministering performances.
>
> Facilitate a discussion about their observations using the questions listed as a guide.
>
> Be sure to add key take aways from your own perspective.

Now THAT'S Amazing

Participant Workbook Page 100

View a video of one of your ministering performances, then answer the below questions.

What story does the choreography tell?
_____
_____

How is that story conveyed in your choice of garments?
_____
_____

How is that story conveyed in your choice of props?
_____
_____

Are you able to detect a mood from the choreography?
_____
_____

Did you notice the execution of small details? List examples.
_____
_____

How did the facial expressions support the choreography?
_____
_____

How did you utilize the musicality in your choreography?
_____
_____

Leaders Note:

Play this video for your group:

https://www.youtube.com/watch?v=eku6HSN613M

Facilitate a discussion about their observations.
Be sure to add key take aways from your own perspective.

	Now THAT'S Amazing	Participant Workbook Page 101

View this video from the show So You Think You Can Dance.
https://www.youtube.com/watch?v=eku6HSN613M

What story does the choreography tell?
_____
_____

How is that story conveyed in the choice of garments?
_____
_____

How is that story conveyed in the choice of props?
_____
_____

Are you able to detect a mood from the choreography?
_____
_____

Did you notice the execution of small details? List examples.
_____
_____

How did the facial expressions support the choreography?
_____
_____

How was musicality utilized in the choreography?
_____
_____

Leaders Note:

Play this video for your group:

https://www.youtube.com/watch?v=m_BiJFmzHbAa

Facilitate a discussion about their observations.
Be sure to add key take aways from your own perspective.

Now THAT'S Amazing

Participant Workbook Page 102

View this video from the show So You Think You Can Dance.
https://www.youtube.com/watch?v=m_BiJFmzHbAa

What story does the choreography tell?
_____
_____

How is that story conveyed in the choice of garments?
_____
_____

How is that story conveyed in the choice of props?
_____
_____

Are you able to detect a mood from the choreography?
_____
_____

Did you notice the execution of small details? List examples.
_____
_____

How did the facial expressions support the choreography?
_____
_____

How was musicality utilized in the choreography?
_____
_____

Leaders Note:

Play this video for your group:

https://www.youtube.com/watch?v=ag2sfN4g7Ns

Facilitate a discussion about their observations.
Be sure to add key take aways from your own perspective.

Now THAT'S Amazing	Participant Workbook Page 103

View this video from the show So You Think You Can Dance.
https://www.youtube.com/watch?v=ag2sfN4g7Ns

What story does the choreography tell?
_____
_____

How is that story conveyed in the choice of garments?
_____
_____

How is that story conveyed in the choice of props?
_____
_____

Are you able to detect a mood from the choreography?
_____
_____

Did you notice the execution of small details? List examples.
_____
_____

How did the facial expressions support the choreography?
_____
_____

How was musicality utilized in the choreography?
_____
_____

| Participant Workbook Page 104 | Now THAT'S Amazing |

Keys to Creating Great Choreography:

1 – Make Your Choreography Tell a Story
It's not enough to motion your arms in the air and spin in a fast circle. To make your choreography more engaging and powerful, it should tell a story. If the music were to stop, or there were no lyrics to your song, would it be possible to discern what the song was about? If this answer is more of a no than a yes, you'll need to practice telling a story through your movement.

2 – Start When the Music Starts
When there is no movement in the introduction, you allow your congregation/audience to divert their attention to something else. Think through the intro portion of the song and include it in your choreography.

3 – The Difference is in the Details
Making your choreography detailed doesn't mean the choreography becomes convoluted or complicated, but it will make it more engaging and passionate. Add detail to your movements, which will sharpen your execution and better deliver your ministry message.

Now THAT'S Amazing

Participant Workbook Page 105

Keys to Creating Great Choreography:

4 – Use Your Entire Body, Including Your Face
Facial expressions that support your choreography and the song's story go a long way. Inversely, the lack of facial expressions (or the wrong ones) go a long way too…just in a direction you don't want to go.

5 – Find a Balance Between Repetition and Variety
Without variety, your routine can come across as mundane, but too much variety will cause your routine to seem all over the map, confusing your audience. Be sure to balance the two for the best presentation.

Leader's Notes and Observations

Now THAT'S Amazing

Participant Workbook Page 106

It's Time to Move!

Review what you wrote from the previous module and review the scenes you wrote for each of your selected songs. Map out your choreography for the song with telling a story in mind. Get on your feet and put your thoughts in motion. Use the below space to take notes if you need to. Do this for each song.

_____

_____

_____

_____

_____

_____

_____

_____

_____

Participant Workbook Page 107

Now THAT'S Amazing

Song #2

_____
_____
_____
_____
_____
_____
_____
_____
_____
_____
_____
_____

Now THAT'S Amazing

Participant Workbook Page 108

Song #3

_____

_____

_____

_____

_____

_____

_____

_____

_____

_____

_____

_____

Participant Workbook Page 109 — Now THAT'S Amazing

Song #4

Now THAT'S Amazing

Participant Workbook Page 110

Song #5

Participant Workbook Page 111 — **Now THAT'S Amazing**

Song #6

_____

_____

_____

_____

_____

_____

_____

_____

_____

_____

_____

_____

Now THAT'S Amazing

Participant Workbook Page 112

Song # 7

Leader's Notes and Observations

Creative Choreography Building Activities

Participant Workbook Page 113

> Leaders Note:
>
> ***Page 114 of the Participant's Workbook asks participants to find and write a scripture related to the module.**
>
> For this exercise, have your dancers find a place on the floor (standing) where they have ample room to move, without colliding with each other. Instruct them to close their eyes* (and keep 'em closed!). You will have to promise them that you won't hit them, poke them, eat their snacks or anything else they might get suspicious about when they close their eyes. Have strips of material on hand just in case you have peekers.
>
> Let them know you are going to call out some words, and they have to express that word in movement. Ask them to think as creatively as they can. Tell them you won't move on to the next word until everyone has made an expression. You may have to wait on a few people to think about their movement, but don't move on until everyone does something.
>
> Continue your list for as many words as you'd like, and you may want to repeat a few. Don't be afraid to challenge your dancers to move beyond just standing! They can kneel, bow, sit, sink, melt, stand on one foot, arabesque, pirouette, and everything in between! Make this suggestion only if you notice that no one is thinking along these creative lines.

Leaders Note:

Once you are done, have dancers share with the group some of the movements you saw, attempting to utilize at least one movement from each person on your team. You can later incorporate those movements in your choreography as needed.

Be sure to watch pay attention to the movements so that no one gets hurt. Walk the room and gently guide dancers who are at risk of running into something or someone.

Variation 1:
Have dancers close their eyes (or use a blindfold) at your discretion. Closed eyes keeps dancers from simply mimicking each other, but forces them to use their own creativity.

Variation 2:
Have dancers work in pairs or small groups.

Variation 3:
Use a metronome and have dancer extend the timing of their movements to last 4 to eight counts.

Variation 4:
Have handy various props and have dancers to utilize them in their expressions.

Motion Word List

Heat	Bored	Small	Happiness	Excited
Prayer	Intense	God	Surrender	Mind
Change	Hurt	Water	Bound	Open
Nervous	Praise	Lift	Fire	Rest
Upraise	Know	Power	Presence	Consume
Jesus	Lift	Fight	Protection	Great
Careful	Stand	Shift	Receive	Spirit
Safety	Seek	Cast	Blood	Savior
Holy	Cry	Press	Thank You	Heart
Healed	Born	Burden	Battle	Mighty
Serve	Strong	Shame	Lord	Prosper
Exalted	Heavens	Tremble	Darkness	Fear
Help	Tears	Majesty	Goodness	Enter
Sleep	Preach	Just	Righteous	Valley
Storm	Cross	Weight	Mercy	Labor
Beneath	Above	Grace	Ocean	Rush
Saved	Cleanse	Sick	Broken	Through
Thirsty	Drink	Keep	Mountain	Fill
Inside	Long	Draw(n)	Complete	Paid
Throne	Earth	Tragedy	Excellent	Struggle
Morning	Forever	Journey	Isolated	Whisper
Shout	Blessing	Comfort	Troubled	Dancing
Word	Hunger	Death	Direction	Majestic

Motion Word List

Love	Peace	Resurrection	Atmosphere
Wonder	Delight	Scared	Worship
Joy	King	Life	Ruler
Stretch	Poor	Together	Conquer
Search	Come	Speak	Holy Spirit
Still	Breath	Victorious	Grateful
Every	Deliver	Faith	Believe
Blind	More	Close(d)	Hear
Take	Fire	Abundance	Suffer
Higher	Crown	Celebrate	Dressed
Cover	Bear	Reach	Scatter
Deep	Pain	Rejoice	Yes
Carry	Glory	Triumph	Follow
Sinner	Nails	Hallelujah	Midnight
Endure	Calvary	Forsaken	Whole
Time	Lonely	Stars	Amazing
Free	Sink	Carry	Give

Leader's Notes and Observations

Creativity Builder
Blind Man, Blind Man Cannot See

Participant Workbook Page 115

Blind Man, Blind Man; Cannot See
You will need to find a place on the floor (standing) where you have ample room to move, without colliding with anyone.

Your instructor will call out some words, and you must express that word in movement. You may even have to close your eyes!

Was this exercise easy?
_____
_____
_____
_____
_____
_____

What did you find challenging about this exercise?
_____
_____
_____
_____
_____
_____

What did you learn and how will you implement it?
_____
_____
_____
_____
_____
_____

Participant Workbook Page 116

**Creativity Builder
Motion Words**

Develop your own Motion Words list for your Creativity Builder exercises. Listen to song lyrics to inspire and assist you if needed.

Leaders Note:

This exercise is similar to Partner Collaboration but it's much more fast paced and requires super quick thinking.
Divide the group into Group A and Group B, then pair a dancer from Group A with a dance from Group B. Have the Person A stand on one side of the room, and Person be stand on the opposite side.

Assign a specific "role" to the dancers in Group A, and a complementing "role" to those in Group B.
Example: Group A = Mother, Group B = Child
Tell the group you will call out "1...2...3...Red Light!" You can call this out as quickly or as slowly as you want. Makes sure that the partners, however are able to reach each other in the three counts. In other words, do not space them so far apart across the room that they aren't able to connect and create their demonstration.

As you call out "1...2...3..." they will need to race to each other and position themselves collaboratively to display their roles, having only 3 count's to do so. When you yell out Red-light, they must freeze their positions. They will NOT have time to discuss with each other the idea for what they will demonstrate, or how they will come together.

Leaders Note:

Once they are frozen, assess their positions, to tweak, correct, or discuss the displays.
Below are some roles to start you off, then you have a Dance Doc to complete, to create your own.

Group A Roles | **Group B Roles**
You have water | You are extremely thirsty
You are running away | You want her to stay
You're the father | Returning prodigal son
You are desperate | You have what she needs
You are providing comfort | You need comforting

**Creativity Builder
1…2…3…Red Light!**

Participant Workbook Page 117

In this exercise, you will be working with a partner. Wait for instructions from your director.

Once you have completed the exercise, write down your favorite role demonstrations.

	Group A Roles	Group B Roles
1		
2		
3		
4		
5		
6		
7		
8		
9		
10		

| Participant Workbook Page 118 | Creativity Builder 1...2...3...Red Light! |

Develop your own Partner Collaborations list for your Partner Collaboration exercises.

	Group A Roles	Group B Roles
1		
2		
3		
4		
5		
6		
7		
8		
9		
10		
11		
12		
13		
14		
15		

Leaders Note:

Play for your group a song that is rich in musicality.
Have your dancers listen to and identify instruments, musical highs and lows, rhythms and syncopation. Discuss what was heard.

Here are example of musically rich songs:

Trans-Siberian Orchestra - Christmas Eve - Sarajevo 12 - 24
- https://www.youtube.com/watch?v=sw0-nhQeqbc

Martha Munizzi - Excellent (Reprise)
- https://www.youtube.com/watch?v=Ai6hRI9ZYy0

Richard Smallwood – Anthem of Praise
- https://www.youtube.com/watch?v=y7Yo2HDxbJo

Have your dancers dance, focusing on the musicality, not the lyrics. Consider having them focus on an individual instrument, or you may want to assign the instruments yourself.

Participant Workbook Page 119

**Creativity Builder
Must be the Music**

Must be the Music

Music is very powerful and can set the tone and mood in an atmosphere. For example, what kind of music do you expect to hear at the below events:

A Child's Birthday Party:
_____
_____
_____

An Adult's Birthday Party:
_____
_____
_____

A funeral:
_____
_____
_____

A wedding:
_____
_____
_____

**Creativity Builder
Must be the Music**

Participant Workbook Page 120

A haunted house:
_____
_____
_____

A church:
_____
_____
_____

A club:
_____
_____
_____

What would your response be if you attended a beautiful summer wedding and there was Halloween themed music playing for the entire ceremony?
_____
_____
_____

How would you react if you attended an adult birthday party and the DJ played nursery rhyme tunes?
_____
_____
_____

Participant Workbook Page 121

**Creativity Builder
Must be the Music**

Your instructor will play a few songs for you. Take notes on what you hear, what mood it creates, and what event you think the song would be appropriate for.

_____
_____
_____
_____
_____
_____
_____
_____
_____
_____
_____
_____
_____
_____
_____
_____
_____
_____
_____
_____
_____

**Creativity Builder
Must be the Music**

Participant Workbook Page 122

Identify and list the titles to 15 songs that are rich in musicality. Share this list with your team.

1.
2.
3.
4.
5.
6.
7.
8.
9.
10.
11.
12.
13.
14.
15.

Participant Workbook Page 123

A Creative Anointing

Creativity doesn't stop with your movement. Expand your thinking to encompass other areas such as your garments (there is an upcoming module on this topic.

Creativity in Garments:
Think of ways you can enhance or modify your dance garments to increase the display of creativity. This could be as simple as changing the color of your leggings or as complex as combining garments to create a different ensemble.

_____
_____
_____
_____

What things can you add to your garment wardrobe?

_____
_____
_____
_____

Facial Expressions

Participant Workbook Page 125

***Page 126 of the Participant's Workbook asks participants to find and write a scripture related to the module.

For thou hast made him most blessed for ever: thou hast made him exceeding glad with thy countenance.

Psalm 21:6

You Look So Much Better When You Smile

Participant Workbook Page 127

The light of my face was precious to them.
Job 29:24

It is important that you remember your face is a part of your body, and participating in the dance ministry should engage your entire body - face included. Facial expressions are God-given, and should be used when appropriate. Some people will say "I just never show my expression." Again, I want to tell you that when God created you, He gave you the natural ability to express your emotions on your face. We just simply learn how to hide them, or attempt to hide them when we feel the need to.

To prove this, consider a baby. A baby naturally smiles when she's happy, scowls when she's upset, widens her eyes when startled or frightened, and so on, and does so out of natural response and reaction. A baby has not learned how to manipulate his or her countenance.

Showing expression is natural and should not be eliminated from Dance/Mime choreography, but should be appropriately demonstrated.

| Participant Workbook Page 128 | **You Look So Much Better When You Smile** |

For each of the expressions shown, write down what you think would be on the dancer's mind if she were to minister with that expression. Also write down in what **instance the expression would be appropriate**. Finally, identify the expression you see most on the faces of your team members when you go forth to minister, and which you deem is most acceptable.

154   TheDanceMinistryManual.com

You Look So Much Better When You Smile

Participant Workbook Page 129

155

| Participant Workbook Page 130 | **You Look So Much Better When You Smile** |

Did You See That? Pantomime Artistry

Participant Workbook Page 131

***Page 132 of the Participant's Workbook asks participants to find and write a scripture related to the module.

And, behold, the glory of the God of Israel was there, according to the vision that I saw in the plain.

Ezekiel 8:4

| Did You See That? | Participant Workbook Page 133 |

Most of the time when we view Mime Ministry, what it typically looks like is a jerky, choppy, exaggerated lip sync of a song. The artistry of mime is not that at all, as outside of ministry, pantomime is performed silently or maybe to an instrumental track.

Miming is actually the art of helping the audience to see something that really isn't there. Have you ever seen a mime pretend to run into a wall, or maybe be trapped inside a box? It wasn't because the movements were jerky or choppy, granted they may have been exaggerated but more importantly, the movement implied the surroundings.

With this in mind, ask yourself if your mime choreography suggests what's happening in your surroundings or is your choreography limited to aggressive pointing and other movements which don't engage the imagination.

Participant Workbook Page 134

What's Your Assessment

What have been your general observations for mime ministry?
_____
_____
_____
_____
_____
_____
_____
_____
_____
_____
_____
_____
_____
_____
_____
_____
_____
_____
_____
_____
_____
_____
_____
_____
_____

Leaders Note:

Play this video for your group, then be ready to facilitate a discussion.

https://www.youtube.com/watch?v=6UhAf3v_uvI

| Participant Workbook Page 135 | **Did You See That?** |

Your Instructor will play two videos for you. After watching them, make an assessment of each mime's performance.

Video One - Larry the Mime Prank

What were the emotions conveyed through his facial expressions?
_____
_____
_____

What communication was conveyed through his body motion?
_____
_____
_____

What if any movements did you notice served no purpose?
_____
_____
_____

What objects did he attempt to have the audience visualize through the implication of motion?
_____
_____
_____

Write down the feedback given at 2:34?
_____
_____

Leaders Note:

Play this video for your group, then be ready to facilitate a discussion.

https://www.youtube.com/watch?v=KKOwuMWBfNQ

Talk about the differences between the two presentations.

Participant Workbook Page 136 — **Did You See That?**

Video Two – Marcel Marceau

What were the emotions conveyed through his facial expressions?
_____
_____
_____

What communication was conveyed through his body motion?
_____
_____
_____

What if any movements did you notice served no purpose?
_____
_____
_____

What objects did he attempt to have the audience visualize through the implication of motion?
_____
_____
_____

What story did his choreography tell?
_____
_____
_____

Leaders Note:

As the team share their assessment of the faces, ask them what about the make up leads them to that assessment. Point out that in most of the pictures, the mime is not really showing much expression at all.

Ask the team to determine which face looks to have the best make up application.

Participant Workbook Page 137

Your Own Notes

| Did You See That? | Participant Workbook Page 138 |

Write your assessment and interpretation of these faces. What mood and tone do they suggest? Would you consider them appropriate for ministry?

_____   _____   _____
_____   _____   _____
_____   _____   _____
_____   _____   _____
_____   _____   _____
_____   _____   _____
_____   _____   _____
_____   _____   _____

Did You See That?

Participant Workbook Page 139

Did You See That?

Participant Workbook Page 140

> **Leaders Note:**
>
> Have your team to think as detailed as possible about executing various activities. Discuss with them how details make a huge difference in execution.
>
> As they share the details of executing the activities with the group, note and point out any steps that were left out.

| | Did You See That? | Participant Workbook Page 141 |

On the following pages you will need to list the details involved for carrying out an action/scenario. The list should be as detailed as you can make it, thinking through every single step. Be sure to consider what things happen before the actual action, as well as what happens after the action. Here is an example.

Action	Details
Pouring and enjoying a bowl of cereal	Walk into the kitchen Open the cabinet Select a bowl Place the bowl on a table Walk across the room Open cabinet to get cereal Place cereal on the table Walk across the room Open refrigerator Look for and get milk Place milk on the table Open cereal box Open plastic bag inside box Shake box to pour cereal Put box down Open and pour milk Put milk down Get a spoon Eat cereal

Participant Workbook Page 142	Did You See That?

Action	Details
Call your dog and take him for a walk	

| Did You See That? | Participant Workbook Page 143 |

Action	Details
Calm a crying baby with a bottle	

| Participant Workbook Page 144 | Did You See That? |

Action	Details
Sing a song for a crowd of thousands of fans	

| Did You See That? | Participant Workbook Page 145 |

Action	Details
Wash, dry and fold a load of laundry	

Participant Workbook Page 146	Did You See That?

Action	Details
Wake up and realize you are late for work/school	

| Did You See That? | Participant Workbook Page 147 |

Action	Details
Fit into a dress/pair of pants that is too small	

| Participant Workbook Page 148 | Did You See That? |

Action	Details
Order and enjoy a meal at a fast food restaurant	

Did You See That?

Participant Workbook Page 149

Action	Details
Put on roller skates for the very first time	

Participant Workbook Page 150	Did You See That?

Action	Details
Lift weights	

Did You See That?

Participant Workbook Page 151

Action	Details
Blow up a bouquet of balloons	

> Leaders Note:
>
> Create scenarios for you team, or have them create them on their own.
>
> Additionally, think of songs that you may already mime, and what actions are expressed in those songs.

| **Did You See That?** | Participant Workbook Page 152 |

Now create your own scenarios, and list the details that will show that action. While the examples you worked on were random, this is a great place to practice tying this into the theme of your songs or choreography.

Action	Details
_____	
_____	
_____	
_____	
_____	

Participant Workbook Page 153

Did You See That?

Action	Details
_____	
_____	
_____	
_____	
_____	

Did You See That?

Participant Workbook Page 154

Action	Details
_____	
_____	
_____	
_____	
_____	

Did You See That?

Participant Workbook Page 155

Action	Details
_____	
_____	
_____	
_____	
_____	

Did You See That?

Participant Workbook Page 156

Action	Details
_____ _____ _____ _____ _____	

Participant Workbook Page 157

Did You See That?

Action	Details
_____	
_____	
_____	
_____	
_____	

Did You See That?

Participant Workbook Page 158

Action	Details
_____ _____ _____ _____ _____	

Participant Workbook Page 159

Did You See That?

Action	Details
_____	
_____	
_____	
_____	
_____	

Did You See That?

Participant Workbook Page 160

Action	Details
_____ _____ _____ _____ _____	

Participant Workbook Page 161

Did You See That?

Action	Details
_____ _____ _____ _____ _____	

Did You See That?

Participant Workbook Page 162

Action	Details
_____	
_____	
_____	
_____	
_____	

> Leaders Note:
>
> Have your team to demonstrate the steps they outlined.
>
> As they execute the activities, note and point out any steps that were left out.
>
> Consider having the group partner or work in small groups to carry out the activities as a group rather than alone.

Did You See That?

Participant Workbook Page 163

Expand on the previous exercise where you listed details for actions/scenarios, by making these actions more expressive. Think of appropriate body or other expressions and facial expressions that increase the demonstration and will help your audience visualize your actions. Here is an example for Enjoying a Bowl of Cereal.

Action	Body/Other Expression	Facial Expression
Walk into the kitchen	Stretch and slump, walk slowly, rub eyes, scratch	Yawn
Open the cabinet	Consider height of cabinet (bend/stretch to show height)	Eyes barely open
Select a bowl	Pick a bowl, then pick a smaller or larger bowl. Show the weight of the bowl in your movement,	Smirk at first bowl choice. Smile and nod at second choice
Place the bowl on a table	Consider height of table when you place the bowl down	
Walk across the room	No longer slumping	Face no longer looks sleepy
Open cabinet to get cereal	Look through other items in cabinet. Lift box and shake to determine amount of cereal in the box	Show pleasure or disappointment with amount of cereal
Place cereal on the table	Consider height of table when you place the box down	
Walk across the room	Body is more awake than at the beginning	

Participant Workbook Page 164	Did You See That?

Call your dog and take him for a walk

Action	Body Expression	Facial Expression

	Participant Workbook Page 165
Did You See That?	

Calm a crying baby with a bottle

Action	Body Expression	Facial Expression

Participant Workbook Page 166

Did You See That?

Sing a song for a crowd of thousands of fans

Action	Body Expression	Facial Expression

Did You See That?

Participant Workbook Page 167

Wash, dry and fold a load of laundry

Action	Body Expression	Facial Expression

| Participant Workbook Page 168 | Did You See That? |

Wake up and realize that you are late for work

Action	Body Expression	Facial Expression

Did You See That?

Participant Workbook Page 169

Fit into a dress/pair of pants that is too small

Action	Body Expression	Facial Expression

Did You See That?

Participant Workbook Page 170

Order and enjoy a meal at a fast food restaurant

Action	Body Expression	Facial Expression

Did You See That?

Participant Workbook Page 171

Put on roller skates for the very first time

Action	Body Expression	Facial Expression

Participant Workbook Page 172	Did You See That?

Lift weights

Action	Body Expression	Facial Expression

Did You See That? — Participant Workbook Page 173

Blow up a bouquet of balloons

Action	Body Expression	Facial Expression

Participant Workbook Page 174

Did You See That?

Now do this exercise for the scenarios you created.

Action	Body Expression	Facial Expression

Did You See That?

Participant Workbook Page 175

Action	Body Expression	Facial Expression

Did You See That?

Participant Workbook Page 176

Action	Body Expression	Facial Expression

Did You See That?

Participant Workbook Page 177

Action	Body Expression	Facial Expression

Participant Workbook Page 178 — **Did You See That?**

Action	Body Expression	Facial Expression

Did You See That?

Participant Workbook Page 179

Action	Body Expression	Facial Expression

Did You See That?

Participant Workbook Page 180

Action	Body Expression	Facial Expression

Did You See That?

Participant Workbook Page 181

Action	Body Expression	Facial Expression

Participant Workbook Page 182

Did You See That?

Action	Body Expression	Facial Expression

Did You See That?

Participant Workbook Page 183

Action	Body Expression	Facial Expression

Participant Workbook Page 184

Did You See That?

Write down any new discoveries, or perceptions about miming you learned in this module.

_____
_____
_____
_____
_____
_____
_____
_____
_____
_____
_____
_____
_____
_____
_____
_____
_____
_____
_____
_____
_____
_____

Did You See That?

Participant Workbook Page 185

Mime Make-Up

White
Why white faces? Mimes use white because not only does it gives a mime a more neutral appearance (thus unifying a group), it enhances facial expression. We've already covered the importance of facial expressions in an earlier segment, and since the white is to enhance expression, it makes no sense to put the white on your face, then forget to use expression.

It is recommended that you use a product called Clown White to cover your face for miming. A quality brand is Ben-Nye. This product is very thick, fairly easy to apply with your finger or with cosmetic sponges, and a little goes a long way!

> **Participant Workbook Page 186**
>
> **Did You See That?**

Additionally, Ben-Nye has make-up products in other colors, such as black for your eyebrows, and red for your lips.

Once you've applied the white base to your face, set it with a face powder. Baby powder will work just fine if you don't want to spend the money on professional makeup, which can be costly.

Shake the powder onto a powder puff, then gently pat it on your face. Another trick is to put the powder into a thin sock, or knee high then lightly pat your face and set the white base. Once you've done this, you will be able to apply the other colors to add detail. If you do not set the white, trying to apply another color over it will result in a blurry, blended mess.

It will take a few rounds of practice to get it your face exactly right!

Black:
The black is mainly utilized for the creation of brows, sometimes for lips, and occasionally for other details such as tears. If you choose to not go with a professional makeup product such as Ben-Nye, an eyebrow or eyeliner pencil also works and may be less expensive.

Red
The red is typically used for lips.

Did You See That?	Participant Workbook Page 187

Cotton swabs work as a great tool for drawing on your brows if you are using a grease type of makeup. They are relatively inexpensive and are plenteous enough for individual applications. Create your brows above your real brows which will again enhance your expressions.

Creative Faces?

Your makeup makes a difference! Before you decide to get creative with your makeup, such as only doing a portion of your face, doing half your face in white and the other half in black, etc., consider what your purpose would be for doing so. Again, if the purpose of mime make up is to enhance your expression, then you have to ask, why would a mime artist only want half, or a quarter of their expression to be enhanced? What imagery does it create that the other portion of the face is not enhanced? How does doing so better communicate the demonstration of the story, or make a more powerful impact? In most cases it does not. Generally speaking, this kind of creative artwork serves no purpose, comes across as being strange and unusual and may set a negative tone for ministry. At best it may just be considered unique, but not impacting.

Also be careful to keep your lines rounded, rather than pointed and jagged, which gives an angry and evil appearance. Often times, rock stars who paint their faces, and are many times alleged to be affiliated with the occult will have dramatic, pointed and sharp angles drawn on their faces.

Participant Workbook Page 188

Did You See That?

Removing Your Makeup

Mime makeup can be easily removed by applying a generous amount of baby oil. Pool some into your hands, apply it all over your face to begin breaking the makeup away. then simply use a washcloth and a gentle soap to remove it completely. Cotton swabs will again come in hand for removing traces of makeup left around the eyes. Apply baby oil directly to the swab, then gently use the swab to remove the makeup.

Make a Mime Kit!

Review and write down the items discussed in this chapter that you will need in your kit, from application to removal, to props.

- _____
- _____
- _____
- _____
- _____
- _____
- _____
- _____

Your Own Notes

Participant Workbook Page 6

Additional Notes:

Leaders Note:

Quick Mime Group Activities:

Build a Statue:
Select a person to be the artist, and the other to be moldable clay. The "clay" starts in a neutral position and allows the artist to slowly mold her into a new position, where the clay is now doing something. The artist should include facial expressions as well.

Have the others attempt to guess the activity in which the clay has been molded to. Talk about the importance of body language.

Sense your surroundings:
This will enhance the group's sensitivity of movement to each other. Have dancers find a space in the room. When you give the word, have them randomly walk around, utilizing the room's space. Then command them to freeze in place for a few seconds. Practice this a couple of times, then have them start and stop at the same time, WITHOUT you giving a command and without talking to each other. As they develop, challenge them to make their communication to move together completely unnoticeable.

Group Objects:
Divide dancers into pairs or small groups. Call out the name of an object and have the dancers create that object out of their bodies, as you slowly count backwards from ten.

Add a Little Something To It - Prop Utilization

Participant Workbook Page 189

***Page 190 of the Participant's Workbook asks participants to find and write a scripture related to the module.

And Miriam the prophetess, the sister of Aaron, took a timbrel in her hand; and all the women went out after her with timbrels and with dances.

Exodus 15:20

Add a Little Something to It!

Participant Workbook Page 191

Prop utilization and can often times add a dynamic to your worship that enhances your choreography. Be sure to test your props in your practice. Sometimes what we envision in our creative minds is not exactly how a particular prop may perform. You will only know if it will work by testing and tweaking. Keep in mind, if you are ministering away from your church, you may not have the same spacing, lighting, aesthetics, etc. as your own church, and the props may not be appropriate or effective. In those cases, if possible, try to view the space where you will be ministering in advance, or choose presentations that utilize simple props if any.

What are some common props you've seen utilized?

- _____
- _____
- _____
- _____
- _____

| Participant Workbook Page 192 | **Add a Little Something to It!** |

Make a list of ten songs that you have already ministered, then ten more that you would like to minister. Listen to each song, engaging your creative mind. Write down what, if any, props could be added to the choreography to better tell the story. When creating your prop list, don't just stop at one or two props; think of as many as you can, then narrow your selection to the prop(s) that will work best.

Song 1: _____

What's the Story? _____
_____
_____
_____

What props would help tell the story? _____
_____
_____
_____
_____

Song 2: _____

What's the Story? _____
_____
_____
_____

What props would help tell the story? _____
_____
_____
_____
_____

| **Add a Little Something to It!** | Participant Workbook Page 193 |

Song 3: _____

What's the Story? _____
_____
_____
_____

What props would help tell the story? _____
_____
_____
_____
_____

Song 4: _____

What's the Story? _____
_____
_____
_____

What props would help tell the story? _____
_____
_____
_____
_____

Participant Workbook Page 194 — **Add a Little Something to It!**

Song 5: _____

What's the Story? _____
_____
_____
_____

What props would help tell the story? _____
_____
_____
_____
_____

Song 6: _____

What's the Story? _____
_____
_____
_____

What props would help tell the story? _____
_____
_____
_____
_____

Add a Little Something to It! — Participant Workbook Page 195

Song 7: _____

What's the Story? _____
_____
_____
_____

What props would help tell the story? _____
_____
_____
_____
_____

Song 8: _____

What's the Story? _____
_____
_____
_____

What props would help tell the story? _____
_____
_____
_____
_____

Participant Workbook Page 196

Add a Little Something to It!

Song 9: _____

What's the Story? _____
_____
_____
_____

What props would help tell the story? _____
_____
_____
_____
_____

Song 10: _____

What's the Story? _____
_____
_____
_____

What props would help tell the story? _____
_____
_____
_____
_____

Add a Little Something to It!

Participant Workbook Page 197

Songs you'd like to minister:

Song 1: _____

What's the Story? _____
_____
_____
_____

What props would help tell the story? _____
_____
_____
_____
_____

Song 2: _____

What's the Story? _____
_____
_____
_____

What props would help tell the story? _____
_____
_____
_____
_____

Participant Workbook Page 198

Add a Little Something to It!

Song 3: _____

What's the Story? _____
_____
_____
_____

What props would help tell the story? _____
_____
_____
_____
_____

Song 4: _____

What's the Story? _____
_____
_____
_____

What props would help tell the story? _____
_____
_____
_____
_____

Add a Little Something to It!

Participant Workbook Page 199

Song 5: _____

What's the Story? _____
_____
_____
_____

What props would help tell the story? _____
_____
_____
_____
_____

Song 6: _____

What's the Story? _____
_____
_____
_____

What props would help tell the story? _____
_____
_____
_____
_____

Participant Workbook Page 200

Add a Little Something to It!

Song 7: _____

What's the Story? _____
_____
_____
_____

What props would help tell the story? _____
_____
_____
_____
_____

Song 8: _____

What's the Story? _____
_____
_____

What props would help tell the story? _____
_____
_____
_____
_____

Add a Little Something to It!

Participant Workbook Page 201

Song 9: _____

What's the Story? _____
_____
_____
_____

What props would help tell the story? _____
_____
_____
_____
_____

Song 10: _____

What's the Story? _____
_____
_____
_____

What props would help tell the story? _____
_____
_____
_____
_____

Leaders Note:

Present these questions when discussing lighting as props.

Dim lights:
What mood is created with dim light?

Black Light:
What mood is created by black light?
What songs can you think of that would be fitting for black light?

Strobe Light:
Lightning is great for portraying storms; what else could it portray?

Glow Sticks:
What other ways can this type of lighting be used?

Add a Little Something to It!

Participant Workbook Page 202

Lighting

Experiment with lighting changes if your sanctuary allows for that. Some sanctuaries are filled with windows, making it near impossible to use lighting effects, unless it's dark outside. Other sanctuaries are closed to outside lighting, making it far easier to explore the possibilities:

- Dimmed Lights - depending on the mood of your song, turning off a light or two may help with conveying your message.
- Black Light - allows white garments to glow in the dark. This is an incredible and impacting illusion.
- Strobe light - This is great when portraying lighting during a storm
- Glow sticks - these can be bought in bulk, along with connector pieces and can easily be attached to garments, or formed into various shapes.

What other prop ideas can you come up with?

The list is endless. Go with what tells the story best. Remember, your garments can also be utilized a props, depending on what they are.

Participant Workbook Page 203

Add a Little Something to It!

Create Your Own

Think of elements that would help you to enhance the story you tell in your choreography. If you can't find those items, create them yourself. You'd be surprised with what you can make with a little hot glue, Styrofoam, feathers, and other materials.

Craft Kit

Having a craft kit is a great idea. Your kit should be filled with general things that you keep on hand to create or repair props. List some items:

- _____
- _____
- _____
- _____
- _____
- _____
- _____
- _____
- _____
- _____
- _____
- _____

- _____
- _____
- _____
- _____
- _____
- _____
- _____
- _____
- _____
- _____
- _____
- _____

| | Add a Little Something to It! | Participant Workbook Page 204 |

Using the Song and Props List you created, review each prop and think about the resources needed to obtain, buy, or create the prop. Some props you may already have on hand. Below is an example.

Prop	Will you buy it? If yes, from where?	Can you make it?	What do you need	Approx. Cost	How often will it be used	Where/How will you store it if needed
Angel Wings	No	Yes	Turkey feathers, hot glue gun, glue sticks, wooden dowels, elastic	$150	Special occasions. Less than 1 time per year.	Attic space at home
Black Light	Amazon	No	Money	$35	1-3 times per year	Dance ministry storage area
Folding Paper Fans	Amazon	No	Money	$10 for 48	As needed	Dance ministry storage area
Folding Chairs	Already have	N/A	N/A	$0	As needed	Church owned

| Participant Workbook Page 205 | Add a Little Something to It! |

Song 1:

Prop	Will you buy it? If yes, from where?	Can you make it?	What do you need	Approx. Cost	How often will it be used	Where/ How will you store it if needed

Add a Little Something to It!

Participant Workbook Page 206

Song 2:

Prop	Will you buy it? If yes, from where?	Can you make it?	What do you need	Approx. Cost	How often will it be used	Where/ How will you store it if needed

Add a Little Something to It!

Participant Workbook Page 207

Song 3:

Prop	Will you buy it? If yes, from where?	Can you make it?	What do you need	Approx. Cost	How often will it be used	Where/How will you store it if needed

Add a Little Something to It!

Participant Workbook Page 208

Song 4:

Prop	Will you buy it? If yes, from where?	Can you make it?	What do you need	Approx. Cost	How often will it be used	Where/ How will you store it if needed

Participant Workbook Page 209

Add a Little Something to It!

Song 5:

Prop	Will you buy it? If yes, from where?	Can you make it?	What do you need	Approx. Cost	How often will it be used	Where/How will you store it if needed

Add a Little Something to It!

Participant Workbook Page 210

Song 6:

Prop	Will you buy it? If yes, from where?	Can you make it?	What do you need	Approx. Cost	How often will it be used	Where/How will you store it if needed

Participant Workbook Page 211

Add a Little Something to It!

Song 7:

Prop	Will you buy it? If yes, from where?	Can you make it?	What do you need	Approx. Cost	How often will it be used	Where/How will you store it if needed

Add a Little Something to It!

Participant Workbook Page 212

Song 8:

Prop	Will you buy it? If yes, from where?	Can you make it?	What do you need	Approx. Cost	How often will it be used	Where/How will you store it if needed

Participant Workbook Page 213

Add a Little Something to It!

Song 9:

Prop	Will you buy it? If yes, from where?	Can you make it?	What do you need	Approx. Cost	How often will it be used	Where/How will you store it if needed

| **Add a Little Something to It!** | | | | | | **Participant Workbook Page 214** |

Song 10:

Prop	Will you buy it? If yes, from where?	Can you make it?	What do you need	Approx. Cost	How often will it be used	Where/How will you store it if needed

Participant Workbook Page 215	**Add a Little Something to It!**

Song 11:

Prop	Will you buy it? If yes, from where?	Can you make it?	What do you need	Approx. Cost	How often will it be used	Where/How will you store it if needed

Add a Little Something to It!

Participant Workbook Page 216

Song 12:

Prop	Will you buy it? If yes, from where?	Can you make it?	What do you need	Approx. Cost	How often will it be used	Where/How will you store it if needed

Participant Workbook Page 217 — **Add a Little Something to It!**

Song 13:

Prop	Will you buy it? If yes, from where?	Can you make it?	What do you need	Approx. Cost	How often will it be used	Where/How will you store it if needed

| **Add a Little Something to It!** | Participant Workbook Page 218 |

Song 14:

Prop	Will you buy it? If yes, from where?	Can you make it?	What do you need	Approx. Cost	How often will it be used	Where/How will you store it if needed

| Participant Workbook Page 219 | Add a Little Something to It! |

Song 15:

Prop	Will you buy it? If yes, from where?	Can you make it?	What do you need	Approx. Cost	How often will it be used	Where/How will you store it if needed

Add a Little Something to It!

Participant Workbook Page 220

Song 16:

Prop	Will you buy it? If yes, from where?	Can you make it?	What do you need	Approx. Cost	How often will it be used	Where/How will you store it if needed

Participant Workbook Page 221

Add a Little Something to It!

Song 17:

Prop	Will you buy it? If yes, from where?	Can you make it?	What do you need	Approx. Cost	How often will it be used	Where/How will you store it if needed

| **Add a Little Something to It!** | **Participant Workbook Page 222** |

Song 18:

Prop	Will you buy it? If yes, from where?	Can you make it?	What do you need	Approx. Cost	How often will it be used	Where/How will you store it if needed

Participant Workbook Page 223

Add a Little Something to It!

Song 19:

Prop	Will you buy it? If yes, from where?	Can you make it?	What do you need	Approx. Cost	How often will it be used	Where/How will you store it if needed

Add a Little Something to It!

Participant Workbook Page 224

Song 20:

Prop	Will you buy it? If yes, from where?	Can you make it?	What do you need	Approx. Cost	How often will it be used	Where/How will you store it if needed

Participant Workbook Page 225

Add a Little Something to It!

Take a peek at this video on YouTube to see what we made when we needed a star for our Christmas presentation:

http://youtu.be/AxyCLgVr1Mc

Materials Used
- 10oz plastic cups
- String of Christmas tree lights
- Clothes Pins (to hold cups together during construction)
- Hot glue gun and glue sticks
- 1.5 foot of ribbon (to suspend)

| Add a Little Something to It! | Participant Workbook Page 226 |

This tombstone was made from two large sheets of Styrofoam cut into shape and carved with a simple kitchen knife. A bit of black paint mixed with water and put in a spray bottle to give it some color, along with some real grass and twigs.

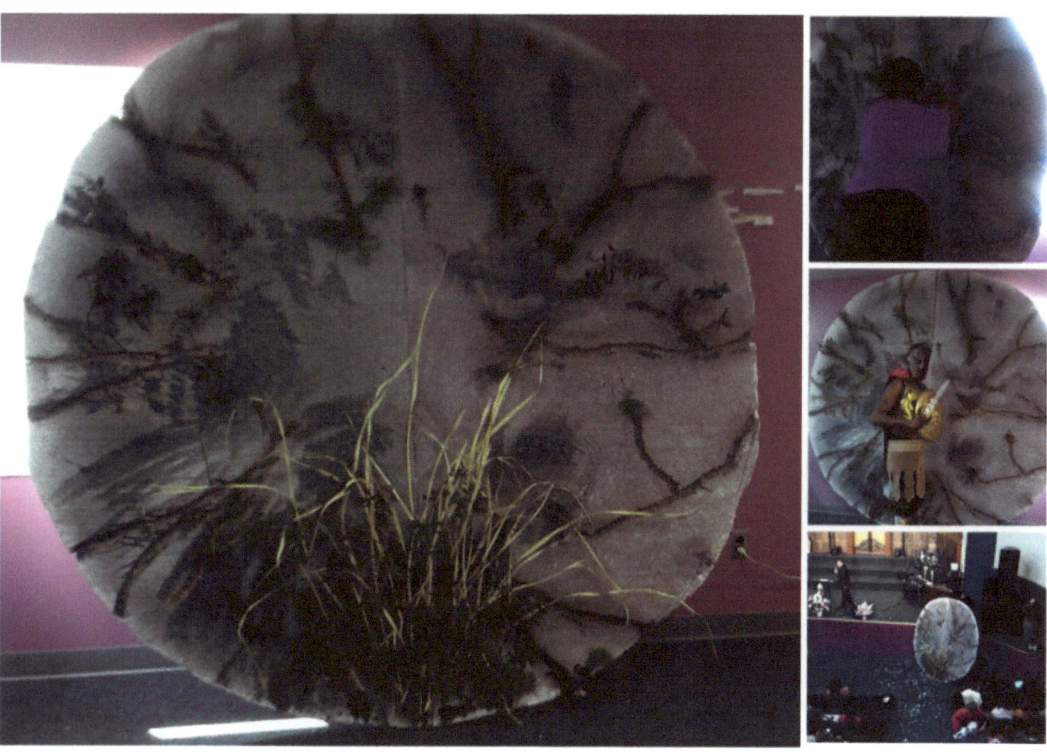

Materials Used:
- 2 sheets of Styrofoam (purchased at Home Depot)
- 1 Small tube of black acrylic paint
- A spray bottle with water
- A large kitchen knife
- Glue gun and glue sticks
- 3 wooden dowels
- Grass and twigs

Add a Little Something to It!

Participant Workbook Page 227

Here are some angel wings that were constructed with turkey feathers, hot glue and wooden dowels.

Materials Used
- Turkey Feathers
- Wooden dowels
- Hot glue gun and glue sticks
- Elastic (to strap to body)

Add a Little Something to It!

Participant Workbook Page 228

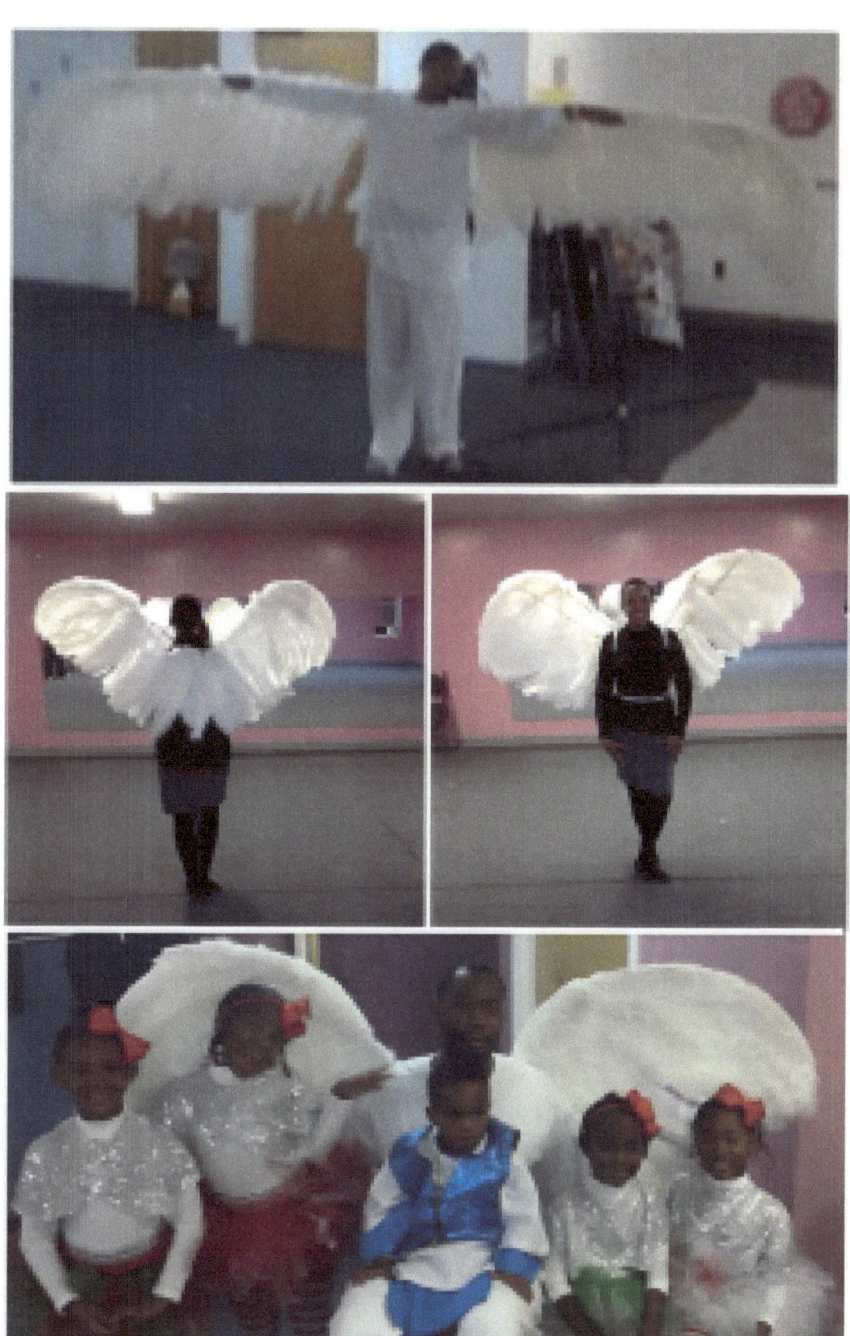

| Participant Workbook Page 229 | Add a Little Something to It! |

These tutus were handmade by the team for our 2013 Christmas presentation.

Materials Used:
- Wide Net-Style Headband
- Strips of Tulle

Getting Dressed for Ministry

Participant Workbook Page 231

***Page 232 of the Participant's Workbook asks participants to find and write a scripture related to the module.

Make sacred garments for your brother Aaron to give him dignity and honor. Tell all the skilled workers to who I have given wisdom in such matters that they are to make garments for Aaron, for his consecration, so he may serve me as priest.

Exodus 28:2-3

Getting Dressed For Ministry

Participant Workbook Page 233

God required specific garments for His priests, as the priests ministered to Him and His people. The dance ministry should have specific garments as well, to be utilized for ministry.

If your budget and/or resources allow, avoid ministering in street clothes, as it vastly diminishes the effect of the ministry. The only exception is that your ministering performance and choreography call for street clothes.

There are several companies now that cater to churches and liturgical dance groups, so much so, that finding garments should not be a barrier for any ministry team. Additionally it is a blessing to have a talented seamstress or tailor to support your ministry, and can make and/or customize garments for you.

Base Garments:
Ensure every team member, male as well as female, is well covered before any dance garment goes on. Some basics would include:

- Black undergarments
- A sports bra (for females)
- An A-shirt (for males)
- Black leggings
- Black leotards

Participant Workbook Page 234

Getting Dressed For Ministry

Make sure that no excessive flesh is visible to include cleavage, midriffs, and the lower back, to mention a few areas.

Mime Garments:
Traditionally, mimes dress in black and white, and often use red as a highlight color. If you choose to be traditional, you can't go wrong with a striped top and black pants, and/or various other combinations of black and white. It is recommended that you only use white gloves however, so that the movement of the hands is properly highlighted, in the same way the white enhances the expression of the face.

There are other garments available in the marketplace that may be conducive to the vision you want to create. That will be a personal choice for your team, however, a good rule of thumb is to ask yourself what purpose does it serve.

Getting Dressed For Ministry

Participant Workbook Page 235

Consistency:

Whatever you decide to wear, strive for consistency in your praise garments. When we examine the leaves of a tree, or the petals of a flower, every leaf or petal is consistent and matches or is cohesive to the others. It would be strange to find a carnation petals  forming within the petals of a blooming rose stem, or a leaf from a rubber tree plant sprouting from an oak tree. We would immediately recognize that something is not quite right about that plant. Even if we are intrigued for a few moments, we recognize that something is out of order; something is amiss. The same thing happens when praise garments are not consistent. It is noticed immediately, and becomes a visual distraction. If there is a variance, make sure there is a purpose to it, or it is a necessary exception.

The same thing happens when praise garments are not consistent. It is noticed immediately, and becomes a visual distraction. To that end consider nail polish, jewelry, hair style and make up choices when it is time to minister.

Participant Workbook Page 236

Getting Dressed For Ministry

Nails: Varied colors and designs and even excessive nail length can be very distracting during ministry and should be avoided. A simple rule is no nail polish, or a simple clear coat. Some like the look of a French manicure, which I agree, looks nice, but only if everyone has one. The same goes for polish on the toes if you're dancing in bare feet.

Jewelry: The same rule is suggested for jewelry; simply do not wear any when you minister; this included wedding rings. I understand that wedding rings/bands are very precious, symbolic, and sentimental, however, another team member who may be unmarried may have a piece of jewelry that she feels is equally precious and sentimental, say for instance, a necklace given to her by her father before he passed away just a few short years ago. It would be completely inconsistent to ask the young lady to remove her necklace, but allow another young lady to keep her wedding jewelry on. Let's not even get into different styles and tastes in accessories. Again, a simple resolve is, no jewelry.

Hair: Dancers should wear hair away from the face, and preferably up or back, and secured. It becomes greatly distracting when a dancer has to jerk her head around trying to remove her hair from her eyes. It is equally distracting when she breaks choreography to use her hand to do the same.

Getting Dressed For Ministry

Participant Workbook Page 237

Even more so, think of how many images you've seen where a female whips her hair around her head in an effort to seduce someone. You don't want to inadvertently create that same type of imagery, or evoke that same emotion, when it can be avoided by securing your hair away from your face.

Makeup: If makeup is worn, it should enhance natural beauty, not draw attention. Keep make up modest and beautifying, not strange and unusual, or overly glamorous. During ministry is not the time to display a new color of bold lipstick, or the mascara that gives you four times the volume and length of your normal lashes. Be beautiful, but moderation is key.

Hygiene Concerns: It is a great idea to keep a "Necessary Basket" handy during your practices and whenever you minister, so that anyone can take care of any unexpected hygiene emergencies. The basket should include items such as deodorant, lotion, and mouthwash, just to name a few.

Participant Workbook Page 238

Getting Dressed For Ministry

Study These Scriptures Take the next several minutes to write out and meditate on these scriptures

Exodus 28:2-4

_____
_____
_____
_____
_____

Leviticus 16:32

_____
_____
_____
_____
_____
_____

Exodus 35:19

_____
_____
_____
_____
_____
_____

Getting Dressed For Ministry

Participant Workbook Page 239

Study These Scriptures Take the next several minutes to write out and meditate on these scriptures

Ezekiel 42:14

_____
_____
_____
_____
_____
_____

Exodus 39:1

_____
_____
_____
_____
_____
_____

Exodus 40:13

_____
_____
_____
_____
_____
_____

Participant Workbook Page 240	**Getting Dressed For Ministry**

It is vitally important that all dancers have great hygiene. To help those that may need assistance with managing this, always keep a Necessary Basket (a collection of toiletry items) readily accessible for your team.

Use the space below to list what items you want to have on hand at all times in your Necessary Basket. Leave nothing out, or else you will be sure to need it! Listed are a few items to start you off.

- Nail polish remover
- Cotton balls
- Panty liners
- _____
- _____
- _____
- _____
- _____
- _____
- _____
- _____
- _____
- _____
- _____

- _____
- _____
- _____
- _____
- _____
- _____
- _____
- _____
- _____
- _____
- _____
- _____
- _____
- _____

The No-Compete Zone

Participant Workbook Page 241

Leaders Note:

***Page 242 of the Participant's Workbook asks participants to find and write a scripture related to the module.**

Facilitate a discussion on ministry and competition.
- Ask your team if they feel that competing is appropriate at any time. If so, when would it be appropriate.

- Ask if they feel it changes the purpose of the performance.

- Ask how would the team feel if they entered a competition, performed at their very best and feel they should have won, but did not. If they express disappointment or discouragement, ask if they feel this same way when they minister in a non competitive environment, but no lives are touched, saved, delivered, healed or changed for the better.

- Have dancer's discuss 1 Corinthians 10:31: Whether therefore ye eat, or drink, or whatsoever ye do, do all to the glory of God.

The No-Compete Zone	Participant Workbook Page 243

Dance and movement ministry has significantly grown over the past twenty or so years. While it has become, and continues to become more widespread, many ministries have become competitive in spirit. Please understand there is not place in ministry for competition. Lives are at stake and God is trusting you and your ministry to reach and minister to those people, not strive after a trophy or prize money.

Ministry is not selfish; it doesn't look for gain or what it can get out of serving. When we position ourselves or our mindsets to outdo each other, we've lost our focus and our purpose.

Here are seven strategies to help you avoid the spirit of competition.

Be clear on your purpose.
_____
_____
_____

Don't compare your ministries to others.
_____
_____
_____

Participant Workbook Page 244 — The No-Compete Zone

Celebrate with other ministries.
_____
_____
_____

Avoid talking about other ministries.
_____
_____
_____

Do not boast and brag. God gets the glory.
_____
_____
_____

Always do your best.
_____
_____
_____

Try to avoid engagements that are competitive in nature. Attend engagements that are ministry focused instead.
_____
_____
_____

Your Own Notes

Participant Workbook Page 245

Participant Workbook Page 246

And the LORD answered me, and said, Write the vision, and make it plain upon tables, that he may run that readeth it.

Habakkuk 2:2

Your Own Notes

Participant Workbook Page 247

Additional Notes:

_____
_____
_____
_____
_____
_____
_____
_____
_____
_____
_____
_____
_____
_____
_____
_____
_____
_____
_____
_____
_____
_____
_____
_____
_____
_____
_____

Participant Workbook Page 248 — **Your Own Notes**

Your Own Notes

Participant Workbook Page 249

While I am certain that some of the course material, you were already familiar with, I pray that this manual has been useful to you and your ministry, and has provided new learnings and perspectives. If it has been helpful to you, please refer a dance ministry colleague.

It's been an honor to serve you, and I would sincerely love to hear from you. Please keep in contact by staying connected:

Facebook - www.Facebook.com/TheDanceMinistryManual
Instagram – TheDanceMinistryManual
Twitter: TheDanceMinMan
Email: Info@TheDanceMinistryManual

Participant Workbooks can be ordered from:
www.TheDanceMinistryManual.com

Silk swing flags can be ordered from:
www.TheDanceMinistryManual.com

May God continue to richly bless you and your ministry!

Kimberly T. Matthews

www.ingramcontent.com/pod-product-compliance
Lightning Source LLC
Chambersburg PA
CBHW041830300426
44111CB00002B/31